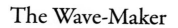

The Wave-Maker

Also by Elizabeth Spires

POETRY

Now the Green Blade Rises (2002)

Worldling (1995)

Annonciade (1989)

Swan's Island (1985)

Globe (1981)

FOR CHILDREN

*I Heard God Talking to Me:
William Edmondson and His Stone Carvings* (forthcoming in 2009)

The Big Meow (2002)

I Am Arachne (2001)

The Mouse of Amherst (1999)

Riddle Road (1999)

With One White Wing (1995)

EDITED BY ELIZABETH SPIRES

Contents of a Minute: Last Poems
by Josephine Jacobsen (2008)

The Instant of Knowing: Lectures, Criticism, and Occasional Prose
by Josephine Jacobsen (1997)

The Wave-Maker

Poems

Elizabeth Spires

W. W. NORTON & COMPANY

NEW YORK   LONDON

For information about permission to reproduce selections
from this book, write to Permissions, W. W. Norton & Company, Inc.,
500 Fifth Avenue, New York, NY 10110

For information about special discounts for bulk purchases, please contact
W. W. Norton Special Sales at specialsales@wwnorton.com or 800-233-4830

Manufacturing by Courier Westford
Book design by Lovedog Studio
Production manager: Julia Druskin

Library of Congress Cataloging-in-Publication Data

Spires, Elizabeth.
    The wave-maker : poems / Elizabeth Spires.—1st ed.
        p. cm.
    ISBN 978-0-393-06659-3
    I. Title.
    PS3569.P554W38 2008
    811'.54—dc22
                                                2008013145

W. W. Norton & Company, Inc.
500 Fifth Avenue, New York, N.Y. 10110
www.wwnorton.com

W. W. Norton & Company Ltd.
Castle House, 75/76 Wells Street, London W1T 3QT

1 2 3 4 5 6 7 8 9 0

for Celia and Madison

Contents

Acknowledgments

The poems in this book first appeared in the following magazines and anthologies:

American Poetry Review: "Translation of My Life"

The Atlantic: "The Wave-Maker"

Bellevue Literary Review: "Curling Willow"

Five Points: "Story of a Soul"; "Essential Snail"; "Photo of You Disappearing"

The Formalist: "A Little Song"

Iowa Review: "White Room"; "A Grave"

Kenyon Review: "Tea"

Metre (Ireland): "Fragment Found in the Garden" (under the title "White Rose")

The New Criterion: "You Have Flown to the Dangerous Country"; "Sunday Morning at the Carmelite Monastery"

The New Republic: "Back Yard"

The New Yorker: "Snail Revisited"; "To a Fog Spirit"; "Nightgown"

The Paris Review: "Badger Disguised as a Monk"

Ploughshares: "Coelacanth"

Poetry: "Snail"; "Sims: The Game"

Poetry Daily (Internet site): "Sims: The Game"; "In a Field"

Redivider: "Grey Garden"

Smartish Pace: "*Zazen*"; "Triptych for Rumi"

Southwest Review: "In a Field"

"Sims: The Game" appeared in *Naming the World*, edited by Nancie Atwell (Heinemann, 2005).

"Snail," "Snail Revisited," "Tea," and "Nightgown" appeared in *Under the Rock Umbrella: Contemporary American Poets from 1951–1977*, edited by William Walsh (Mercer University Press, 2006).

"Brown Bird" was published as a limited edition poetry broadside by the Baylor Poetry Festival.

"To a Robin in Lent," "Fragment Found in the Garden," and "Bloated Haiku" appeared in *Poetry Speaks 2006 Calendar* (Sourcebooks, Inc.).

"Photo of You Disappearing" appeared in *Poetry Speaks 2008 Calendar* (Sourcebooks, Inc.).

"Tea" appeared in *Poetry Calendar 2006* (Alhambra Publishing, Belgium).

"Back Yard" appeared in *Poetry Calendar 2007* (Alhambra Publishing).

"The Wave-Maker" appeared in *Poetry Calendar 2008* (Alhambra Publishing).

The author would like to thank Jill Bialosky for her continued support and encouragement and Goucher College for a sabbatical that provided time to work on these poems.

I

In that melodious silence, something came back to her that had lain dumb and dead ever since the old, innocent undergraduate days. The singing voice, stifled long ago by the pressure of the struggle for existence, and throttled into dumbness by that queer, unhappy contact with physical passion, began to stammer a few uncertain notes. Great golden phrases, rising from nothing and leading to nothing, swam up out of her dreaming mind like the huge, sluggish carp in the cool water of Mercury. One day she climbed up Shotover and sat looking over the spires of the city, deep-down, fathom-drowned, striking from the round bowl of the river basin, improbably remote and lovely as the towers of Tir-nan-Og beneath the green sea-rollers. She held on her knee the loose-leaf note-book....

Then, with many false starts..., returning and filling and erasing painfully as she went, she began to write again, knowing with a deep inner certainty that somehow, after long and bitter wandering, she was once more in her own place.

—Dorothy L. Sayers, *Gaudy Night*

The Wave-Maker

There was intricate machinery involved & a powerful desire
    to make it all move. It had been easy then to stand waist-deep
in the waves & will the world into existence, sea, sky, & cloud,
    the ever-changing elements, moving & robed, like characters
on a stage delivering their lines. Or so she had thought at the time.

That was some years ago. She is older now & occasionally returns
    to inspect the charming, antique machinery, all flywheels & cogs,
surprised that it still works. And notices that on a day like today
    the waves are a colorless color that no word exists for.
She will have to do something about that, she thinks, before
                        memory fails her.

Down on her knees, she lets the old familiar rollers wash her clean,
    & sighing, takes in all the changes since she has last been.
Salt stings her eyes. As if on wires, a gull stalls in the day's crosswinds. .
    Down the beach, a girl, small as the dot on an *i*, is waving
& waving, but the wind takes her words, the waves drown out
                    whatever it is she is saying.

Tea

The road is dust,
and the town is dust,
and even my mother
is dust. But here,

set back among the pines,
a teahouse long and low
where we sit like ancients,
cradling lacquered cups.

Outside, the storm of afternoon.
The dust of existence.
Then the storm passes.
The bamboo shines.

For years what pursued us?
What did we pursue?
Now we are *here*,
in a teahouse of the mind

where a cherry tree blooms
and passes into summer,
where autumn blazes up,
and then the snow, falling

with a stillness that fills
my heart like a cup
in the moment before
the tea is poured.

My friend, sit with me
for a little while.
Let us cleanse ourselves
of the dust of existence.

Snail

I watch you   traverse   the long green table
your trail slick & shiny   then pluck you up
& hold you   wet & glistening   in my open hand

You are a dusky brown   your mottled shell attached
by a wrinkled skinlike mantle   to the rest of you

Touched   your eyes   on long tentacles
retract   & you have two shorter lower tentacles
that feel the ground in front of you   first one
then the other   up & down   carefully they touch the ground

Like someone   feeling her way along   a pitch-black corridor
with no way of knowing   where she is going
like me   perhaps

Your radula   spiked & ragged black mouthhole
tears up & chews   chalk & lettuce   that is all
you need   chalk & lettuce!

For you there is no fight   or flight
startled   you contract into your shell & wait
for Danger to tire   & walk away

A slow-going-forward   a staying-very-still   that is you
speechless creation that leaves me   finally   speechless

Sometimes   I cannot   bear the world
the beauty & perfection of a snail   created
by the same Creator   who created   me

But we are different   you are lowly & humble
you have grace & compression   whereas   I am awkward
& huge   & not humble   forgive me

Do you see me?   is the world seen
from your wary waving eye stalks   a perfect circle?
you see ahead of   & behind you   a thing
I cannot do   do you too   feel terror?

I   monster that I am   bow down before you

Snail Revisited

I want to say   everything there is to say   about you
how you slept   on the ceiling of a plastic salad box
how   sometimes   one eye tentacle   swiveled & stretched
looking   updown   northsouth   eastwest   your eye
meeting mine   curiously   the other   a separate sleepy creature
slow to wake   & follow   the effect   extraterrestrial
once   late at night   the house so still   I heard a sound
it was you   ravenous   unstoppable   eating a carrot strip
I confess   I too   have known such hunger
you were companionable   undemanding   but in December
you died without   ceremony   for days I wasn't sure
I waited for you to resume   movement   to climb clear walls
to eat your lettuce   but No   you were dead
& I   pallbearer of one   carried you   outside
where no sun wind rain   could restore you   the worst
I won't tell   (what Death will do to the body)   finally
you were only   a shell   a monument   a memory
I buried in the herb garden   where your glistening minerals
leach into dark soil   & now   I want to know:
what is your shape   & where is your spirit?
are you leafy?   fragrant?   do you flower?
a balm to butterfly and bee?   then go to seed?
times passes   it is midsummer   & I am alive
& done with Death   until the next time   it happens

A Small Voice Asks Some Large Questions

What if there is no quiet place
where the heart can sit?

No little room somewhere, no
chair, no window with a view?

What if there is no sea to soothe?
No mountains rising in the distance?

What if the words that anchor me
to you, and here to there, all disappear

and all that's left is noise and glare,
a scorched and brutal plain where

the heart must stand like a child
who knows it must not cry or complain,

it must not!, while overhead birds,
big black ones, keep circling and circling?

You Have Flown to the Dangerous Country

You have flown to the dangerous country,
how easily you have left this life behind,
this street, this quiet city street,
where letters arrive each day dependably,
where trees make a canopy in summer,
and winter, it is winter now, possesses a cold clarity.

But in the place where you are there is heat,
there is hunger, and the trees have been cut down,
and dogs, there must be dogs, slink out of the night's
blackness, teeth bared, and the sound of drumming penetrates
your sleep even when there are no drums. And slowly,
you begin to forget the words we are used to saying here,
they speak another language there, a language that has no place
for words like *snow* and *safety*, a language I will never know
because I have never been to the dangerous country,

                                and I do not think I will go.

I think of a tear in a curtain, a jagged man-high tear,
that you step through easily, without a glance backward,
because you are drawn to the dangerous country,
to the need and the want and the hunger,
and to something more that I cannot name.
I feel such a distance, such an unreality,

when I think of you in the dangerous country,
with the heat and the dust and the dogs,
the drums and the knives, the nightmares and the screams.

But I tell myself there must be birds and flowers,
rare flame-colored exotica surrounding tiny pastel houses
that a child might draw, there must be children flying kites,
running along a curving shore where watercolor waves
wash up in shades of ultramarine, there must be
painters painting paintings of it all, and laughter
and singing, because people laugh and sing everywhere,
                                    O tell me that they sing.

Do the people there, do they ever ask you
what it is you mean by *winter* and by *snow*,
by *safety* and by *silence*? Do you try to explain?
And then I begin to wonder what it is to be safe,
do I feel safe here, and is there safety anywhere,
as I move through the rooms of this house, drawing the curtains,
the street so quiet now, and twilight coming on.

To a Fog Spirit
on Halloween

Made up and masked, you stream into the night,
your cape floating like gossamer behind you,
the moon illuminating what you are and are not:
a cool customer, slippery as quicksilver.

I cannot fathom you exactly, though I try to.
Lately, I've noticed you're all about change,
change and silence. And you have properties:
you expand and contract, filling whatever

space you're in, or self-contained as a cat.
Some mornings, impersonating one of *us*,
you wake, dress, eat, then vanish out the door,
the room suddenly too silent, the day clear as a bell.

  I remember a May morning twelve years ago,
  before you were *you*, when I woke to a landscape
  wiped clean as a blackboard and knew you were hiding
  inside a stillness different from any I had ever known.

  And that night in January, after our long journey,
  when we were almost *there*, and the bridge to the island
  disappeared, and we pushed on anyway (did we have a choice?)
  into black foggy bottomless space and didn't fall—

O fog spirit, are you a magician?
How did you do *that*?

Does fog beget fog?
No, you have a mother and father.
So creep back to this house
and with a hand solid as my own
rap *hard!* three times on the door,

      and when it opens, as it will,
      step through the portal and change,
      change back into my daughter again.

Badger Disguised as a Monk

a Japanese netsuke

Deception is necessary. Disguises, too.
When I wrap this cloak around me,
I change into a barefoot, pious fellow
who cries out softly in the darkness,
                    Alms! Alms!
to you and you and you.

The night is calm and cool.
The road is a silver spool
that I must follow as footprints
follow me, dogging whatever it is that I am.

                    What am I?
I am Badger, all snout and paws and appetite.
I am always hungry.

All motion is forward for a soul
with a pockmarked, bitten past.
But I will not look back! I will not!

My tongue, like a clapper on a bell,
rings the word again,
                    Alms!
O who will fill my palm with change? O who?

I shall say a prayer to the Moon
because even a badger prays now and then:
> *O Silver Sliver,*
> *shine down on me and change me*
> *so that I am what I am,*
> *not two things, no, not two!*

But the Moon never answers.
It grows smaller as it ascends,
as if someone or something were eating it.
I understand such hunger.

Troubadour at a Fork in the Road

Grey my hair now, grey,
I sing of better days
when, with a *hey-ho, hey-ho,*
gaily I strode out into the world
to sing my songs to any ear that listened.

Three moments I remember:
the first when the broad road forked
and would not tell me, no, which way
I was to go, and so, with a *hey-ho, hey-ho,*
I stood in the vise of left and right,
yes and no (and stand there still),
as rain rained down, ice held me fast.
O how many ticking clocks were lost or died
while I, with a *hey-ho,* tried to decide
which way to go? And still I do not know.

The road swerved and narrowed,
pulling me into a wood too wide to circle
roundabout, and there I found,
in thorn and briar, there was no turning back.
And so boots ran (are running still),
past shadows worse than any tooth or talon.
How long did that running take?

Fear is no measure, and when I reached
the other side, I found, with a *hey-ho, hey-ho,*
that all my rhymes were shadowed.

And finally I came to the sea,
the wide glittering sea, where grey-green waves
moved just for me (or so I thought),
and sat myself down on a pebbled beach
where, with a *hey-ho, hey-ho,* I piled stones
in a circle around me, not caring for the morrow.
Like an idiot child, I piled my pretty stones,
knowing the waves would knock them down,
and now I ask you, why, o why-o,
in all my wandering was that my happiest day?

Road, forest, sea, the years have grasped me,
greyed me, thrown me down on a stony shore
like a ragged, half-drowned castaway,
and still I do not know, though I sing
hey-ho, hey-ho, just what the journey means.

Story of a Soul

Light. Light. Light. Light. Light.
Streams into her rented room.
A single smallish room, not even a closet,
that's all she cares to live in.
In one corner, a narrow cot
with a nail hammered into the wall above it
where she can hang her nightgown (or is it a dress?).
On the table opposite, a bone china plate
flanked by a spotless linen napkin and heavy old sterling,
embossed with a double "S," without a speck of tarnish on it.
But she eats like a bird when she eats at all—
one oyster perhaps, or a single green grape
washed down by a splash of *vin blanc*—
amusing herself while she does by scribbling
brief, enigmatical entries into her notebook:
>   *Spent the morning writing postcards to G. Didn't send.*
>   *Am I on the right path? Identity crisis!*
>   Or, *Slept all day. Woke up wondering if B. was right,*
>   *that I am insubstantial. Groundless worry? Or not?*
The journal's deliberately cryptic.
Her *real* autobiography, the one going on inside her,
would be as thick as WAR AND PEACE
but will never be written—she keeps a tight rein,
deplores the trend to *confess*. But, oh yes,
she's had her wild nights (hasn't everyone?),

careening around the room like a bat out of Hades.
Or worse, cast down on the floor, limp as an old rag rug.
It was always (no surprise) about LOVE.
Let the word be banished from the English language!
For now, she prefers her nunnish quietude.
Prefers letters to phone calls.
Would like to disconnect the doorbell.

And if an imagined visitor—her landlady perhaps—
were to ask, *But what exactly do you do all day?*
she would deflect the question as she always has.
And once whoever it was had left, she'd resume
her favorite pretend game, the one
where she's the mistress of a grand house,
the owner gone on a long, eternal trip.
Thinking about it, she smiles and plucks at the hem
of her flimsy dress (or is it a nightgown?)
and begins to quietly dust, then wipes all the windows
to a sheer, clear transparency,
until everything is immaculate.

Nightgown

To be inhabited.
To float from room to room
raving, waving my arms.
To be tossed by unfamiliar dreams,
and then to lie limp and slack on the bed.
To be folded, without a thought,
and put in a dark drawer.
Or to hang in a closet, shapeless as a sack,
knowing the terror of form dissolving into formlessness.

    Someone is inside me.
    Someone is continually dreaming
    dreams not my own
    so that I am pulled this way and that!

I have always been attracted to the moon.
To a place where I shiver but do not freeze.
And although I, unlike you, must make do
without head or heart, I can imagine a future
you cannot: where, filled with a wild winter emptiness,
I fly over a streaming patchwork countryside
to see what has so far eluded me:
the white world written on with white writing!

II

Sims: The Game

a popular computer game explained by a child

In some ways it's Life   Real Life
    in some ways Yes   in some ways No

You design the people   they can be
    outgoing   nice   playful   active   neat
    but you can't make them be everything
    if they are neat   they will clean up after themselves
    (charisma is when they talk to themselves
        in front of a mirror)

Adults never get older   & old people can do
    anything young people can do
Adults don't have to have jobs   they can cheat:
    push the rosebud & money appears

    Job objects   like pizza ovens   earn you money
        or you can be   an extra in a movie   a soldier
        a doctor   an astronaut   a human guinea pig

Children get older slowly   every day they get a report card
    children can live in the house without adults
    (a family is anyone who lives in the house with you)

Everyone gets skill points:
    for chess   painting   playing the piano
    gardening   cooking   swimming   mechanics
    (when you get points a circle above your head
        fills up with blue)

& there are goals   not to run out of money   not to die
    & to buy more stuff for the house
    (like a pool table   or an Easy Double Sleeper Bed)

Adults can get married   but it's hard   to get married
    You tell them to propose but they can't   make the decision
    on an empty stomach   or they've just eaten   & are too tired

To have a Baby   click Yes or No   & a baby carriage rolls up

Everyone has to   eat   sleep   go to the bathroom   etc.
    if they live alone   & don't have friends
    they get depressed   & start waving their arms

If you give them Free Will   you don't have to keep track of them
    but it's strange what they'll do:
    once a player fell asleep under the stairs standing up

    & sometimes they go into a bedroom   that isn't theirs
    & sleep in the wrong bed   then you have to tell them:
    Wake up! That is not your bed!

If they are mad   they stomp on each other   or put each other
     in wrestling holds   but no one gets hurt

There are different ways to die:
     you can drown in the pool
     if you swim laps for twenty-four hours
     (the Disaster Family all drowned in the pool
     except the little girl   who kept going
     to school after they died   she was perfect)

& the stove   or fireplace   or grill
     can set the house on fire:
          once there was a fire in the kitchen
          eight people rushed in
          yelling *Fire! Fire!*   & blocked the door
          so the firemen couldn't get through
          (after that everyone had to study cooking
          now there are less accidents)

If you have Free Will   you can starve or drown yourself
     then you wander around as a ghost
     until another player agrees   to resurrect you

In some ways it's Life   Real Life
     in some ways Yes   in some ways No

Translation of My Life

I remember the past.
Before there were poems.
I was eight. The world
simple as a primer.
I lived in a small town
far from the ocean.
Home, then school,
then home again,
back and forth
on my blue bicycle.
In the summer, a blue pool,
white clouds sailing over,
and a song playing
on the jukebox.
Always the same song.
Then fall, with its burning
leaves. Thanksgiving.
Christmas. Over and over.
There are photographs,
yellow and crumbling,
to prove what I say.

Imagine: a town
in the same universe as this one,
with the same physical laws,

but no poets, no poetry.
No scribbling hands up late
at night writing words
they believed would save them.
No noisy fluttering pages
to disturb the peace
of the dreaming populace.
Understand, I was only a girl
living the days as they came.
I did not know then I would leave.
Though I had a secret
I did not tell and will not ever,
I did not know I would leave.

White Room

White room, you've seen me as no one has seen me.
You've listened and said nothing
when I've come to you asking, *Why?*
But still I wonder, should I speak to you like this,
as I never speak to others, or should all be left unsaid?
For too long I've avoided your implications.

Did I create you? The blank white walls,
the warped floorboards that waver and run in all directions,
the high windows through which the world shines,
through which I peer helplessly like a child,
the scene pulling at me the way the moon tugs at water,
                                        makes tides?

Do you exist when I'm gone?
Does the view from the window change
when no one is there to look out of it?
Do dust motes whirl and spin in the light,
or is stasis the only rule?

I had a dream that won't leave me:
I stood on the prow of a ship
in a timeless northern twilight,
the passage ahead narrow and icebound,

the world *gone,* fallen away,
one frozen thought remembered upon waking:
Now I am alone for the first time in my life.

After such a night, I open the door.
Again I ask, Who speaks and who listens?
Is your silence an answer? A mirror?
Is the interior in which I move yours or my own?

In a Field
monosyllables

Like stones
in a field.
Small. Large.

There to be used.
To make walls.
To be thrown.

To be held
in our hands.
Light as air.

Or a big thing
that weighs
us down.

I can hide on
the dark side
of this one.

Or tell all.
When I do,
it is not a game.

I pick one up.
Which one is it?
you ask.

I will not tell.
Come here, I say,
and you will see.

You pick one up.
Then I do. Then you.
Then me. Soon

the field is clear.
We have used
each one.

Now
there is
only silence.

A Little Song

A little corner of the mind
where sun is sieved to shadow.
A little corner of the mind
where plays a little song.

A song conceived in autumn,
by changes in the garden.
You sit among the fallen.
Leaves blow around your chair.

It's cold there, getting colder,
and the bare tree looks so bare.
You sit alone in shadow
and hear what no one hears:

The stillness of still water,
the silence of no sound,
the sorrow of white paper,
the circle that is round.

What good to try to tell them,
those who have never been there,
about a corner of the mind
where plays a little song?

Fragment Found in the Garden

The sun-drenched beetle with a rainbow on its back,
splayed and luxuriating on the wide white petal—
is that what our life could be?

Us, arms outstretched, prone
and petaled on a pillowed world?

Starved and drowning, I kneel to gather
white petals the wind has scattered.

Zazen

to a cricket

On the day of the hurricane,
  when the sky was a violent violet,
    and the birds had vanished into thin air,
      and the trees were bent prostrate to the ground,
    I found you in the basement, still and shaken.
  Then you skittered away sideways and quickly
disappeared under the washing machine.

Nights now, when I bring down the laundry,
  I see you kneeling on the cold hard floor,
    a monk without a mat. It's warm enough, yes,
      but what do you eat? Drink?
    Do you conjure miracles, small ones, in the dark?
  Moment to moment, does your *zazen* preserve
this house, and all within, from destruction?

How speechlessly you go about your business!
  You seem to need nothing, nothing
    except a place, a space to be quiet in.
      Me. You. I. Thou.
    All categories have begun to disappear.
  You are trying to teach me something.
What, I'm not yet sure.

Bloated Haiku

Minnow, abandon your nibbling illusions. Stop preying on tiny imaginations. Swell and grow into the pond's overlord, a fat fish silently devouring all. Release us from the tyranny of the small!

Coelacanth

Once thought to be extinct . . .
lives at depths of up to 1500 feet . . .
dies of shock when brought to the surface . . .
almost nothing is known about it . . .
                    —*National Geographic*

I saw you in a book: bubble-eyed and staring,
mouth spookily aglow with a sourceless yellow light.

Extinct, you cruised among cold silences
until a hand roughly hauled you out of your element,

and for a moment you lived, only to die again,
in shock at a world too bright, too dry, too thin.

Mute, you speak volumes: the weight of water pressing
on you like an enormous question, your ancient saucer eyes

peering, constantly peering, through ragged curtains of Time.
What, what do you see? *O tell me, tell me, tell me.*

You and I, we live in depths profound and ceaseless,
we swim against cold currents until, netted

and gasping, we are shocked to find out
not what we are, but what we have never been.

Essential Snail

Slow.
That is the first thing
you should know
about me.
I'm slow.

~

Things I cannot do:
I cannot sing.
I cannot jump.
I cannot fly.
But why would I want to fly?

~

(To sing would be good
but who would listen?)

~

A few definitions:

~

House: a leaf over my head.

~

House: myself.

~

House: what I'll leave behind.

~

I confess: I,
like you, have written
a poem or two.
My epic?
    To tra-
    verse the
    peri-
    meter.
    To strad-
    dle the
    edge. And
    not to
     f
       a
        l
        l
         .
          .
           .
            !

~

Do you want
to hear a beautiful word?

Are you listening?
Are you *really* listening?

S l i m e.

~

Yesterday
dew on the leaves.
Today
dew on the leaves.
Tomorrow
dew on the leaves.
Is it enough?

~

Cloaked in myself,
I've read the Metaphysicals.
By being, just being,
I pray.
Would Herbert say
I am a snail "well-drest"?

~

Days and nights!
Days and nights!

Moon and sun
whirling across

the sky, and I,
little and low,

part of it all!

~

One way or another,
we all die.

Already, I see
how it will end:
Love, divine,
unknowable,
will pierce me
with an arrow.

I'll lie there,
completely finished,

a slain snail.

~

I watch you
watching me.

You watch me
watching you.

Eye to eye,
I'm at your mercy.

~ ~ ~

III

Love bade me welcome: yet my soul drew back...

—George Herbert

Christmas Eve Morning

Tennessee

Slam! on the sun porch window, and then again, *Slam!*
Outside, a broken cardinal lies on the zigzag brickwork
of the patio, and there in the bushes, a second faintly stirs,
bleeding from the beak, then it, too, is gone.
Held in our hands, they are warm, warm, warm
but dead. One must have been madly chasing the other,
flashes of red flying, darting, keeping up the pace,
until, with a *Slam!*, death put an end to things.
A different trajectory would have saved the second
but left it alone, too solitary, as the other's crimson soul
escaped and drifted, like a puff of smoke, up over
a muted grey-green landscape of field, ridge and hill.

We will die, we are sure of it,
but if we came back, which we are not sure of,
what would be better than this cardinal life, at home
in every season? We live our lives (for the most part)
glassed-in, warm, not hungry, watching, yet somehow
disbelieving, what could (and will) befall us with a *Slam!*
The day is overcast but warm, the mood reflective,
as morning segues at a gravid pace into afternoon,
then into a night of unseasonable thunderstorms,
and then (held breath) . . . it is Christmas. Christmas.

The sun has come out, everything is shining and gleaming,
and there is no mistaking transparency—that glassy wall
between us and them—for air or emptiness.
And now is what we see in the back yard a sort of miracle
or simply the way things are? Two cardinals multiplying
into three, then four, until there are a dozen or more . . .
not resurrection exactly, but a bright fluttering continuance
that does and does not console. The eye cannot count
or track these flashes of red appearing
and disappearing in the trees, darting hungrily
around the birdfeeder, but for now alive, alive, alive.

Sunday Morning at the Carmelite Monastery

My breath,
on this January morning,
a small white cloud

as shivering, I step
into the room of light.
There, on the bare table,

the plate of bread, the cup.
I have come to sit quietly.
To be filled up.

Advent is passed,
the old Nativity
both mystery and fact.

We felt its approach,
peered like curious children
into the bright cave

where the miracle happened.
And now winter, the pilgrim
soul tracking deeper

into snow, unsure
of where to go. Prayers,
for those who pray,

fly silently up
to the vaulted ceiling.
Some, the lucky ones,

pass through, while others
must idly stay and stay.
My thoughts adrift,

I am pulled back
to this moment by a voice
not my own saying,

Today is the first Sunday of ordinary time . . .

The Snowy Day

The last time I saw you, we met for coffee on a snowy day.
Outside the window of the coffee shop, the snow fell silently

& heavily, the traffic on Coldspring Lane blurred & vague,
each car a cumbersome dream vehicle plowing comically into eternity.

But there you were, real as day, drinking a real cup of coffee.
You were back from India, you had slept for two days, the coffee

tasted wonderful, you said. You had flown to a mountain monastery
to find in prayer & silence what you could not find in the everyday,

taking only a few books, a change of clothes, because for too long you
had carried your life like two suitcases heavy enough to kill you.

When it snows, everything is light & dark at the same time. Black coffee
in a white cup, the hours leaked away, until our cups were empty,

the afternoon gone. Then a kiss on the cheek, a door opening out
into the cold, & I was walking away, up a slippery snowy hill
    nothing at all

like your mountain & so little to hold onto. That night the snow fell
& fell & fell, erasing every landmark, quieting the world for a while.

Later, after you died, I had a dream. The phone was ringing.
It was you, your voice, on the other end of the line, laughing

as you said, "Beth, it's Greg. I'm in the hospital. I'm not dead."

Grey Garden

If, one morning, after many hints and premonitions,
you wake to a seasonless season, a grey garden
where nothing lives or dies because nothing
changes, and the only action left is in inaction,
make a place for yourself among these fallen leaves.
Imagine a tree, once high and mighty, now felled
by catastrophe. How something is slowly breaking it down
until it crumbles at the merest touch, its form collapsing
inward. Its only hope, if hope is wise, to come back
as a speechless blade of grass, or one of those flowers
with bowed heads, a snowdrop pushing up through snow.
Time is a construct. You must not think about time.
Lie very still and do not mind the cold or count
the nights. You will know you are part of the scenery
when green shoots push up around your heart,
and small chattering birds make you their careless perch,
and even the insects have something to say
about your situation as they hum and whisper,
part of the earth, the earth, the earth,
and this grey garden comes back to life again.

To a Robin in Lent

You were the first one back,
the first one back.

You clung to a bare black branch,
your habit to choose Sundays in March,
wind whirling around you,
sky grey as a shroud, and wet,
to sing to the flowers, not there yet.

You were not loud.
No, not at all.
But you knew what you were doing.

Brown Bird

Brown bird, where did you come from?
You are brown, brown as a monk's cowl,
brown as an old brown shoe,
brown as the earth the spade turns over.
Brown, not black, in winter's patchy light.

There you are in the garden.
The trees are bare as you alight,
wings aflutter, a brown word
hopping carelessly along,
your two splayed feet
imprinting stone after stone.
Now you fly off. And now return
to drink a drop here, there,
to hang on a twisting vine
that climbs the garden wall.

Brown bird, your element is air,
but where are *my* wings? Where?
I am heavy today, heavy,
and have no tune or tone,
no light or life to share.
But do not leave just yet.
I pray you, do not leave.

Côte d'Azur

In Biot, where the glassmakers live,
I found the house of my dreams, *Clos Mon Rêve*,
its low blue door half-hidden under a stone archway.
It was early. No one was up yet.
Through a gauzy curtain I saw,
or thought I saw, rough whitewashed walls,
a sleeper wound round and round in sheets,
dreaming of nothing, dreaming of glass,
liquid and molten, waiting to be
shaped into a vessel, given form.

That afternoon, I swam, freeing myself
from myself, the water a glassmaker's dream
of blue and darker blue struck and shattered
by the sun into ten thousand shining particles.
I swam, then pulled myself, hand over hand,
up out of gravelly shallows onto land,
like a creature intent upon evolving.

On Friday the chapel in Vence was closed,
but a nun who lived next door unlocked the gate
and let us in. Inside, Christ carried the Cross,
fell, rose again, a black-and-white tableau sketched
by Matisse, after long reflection, "in a moment."

All moments are one moment, she said,
as light from the windows fell in blue pools
on the floor, and words welled up in me:
How is it that though you do not sin, you sin?
How is it that though you believe, you do not believe?

A Grave

I can't stay any longer in a world of death . . .
—*Emily Dickinson*

Moss reaches up.
Touches letters on stone.
A century does its work.
A name, a date, worn down.

The fence makes a space
for you to lie in.
Dead you will never
have to die again.

On an August afternoon,
they carried you
out the back door.
Mother, Father,

waiting here for you.
Now *the mind alone
without corporeal friend*
will tell how moss

reaches up,
how a white flower
lies pressed in a book,
and a moth, vested

in black, settles
weightless on this stone,
pauses for a moment,
then flies on.

Curling Willow

for Josephine Jacobsen (1908–2003)

—I can still get there if I try: it's through the glass doors,
then down the long hallway on the left. Inside, it is always
late afternoon, the bucket of ice set out, the cork on the champagne

popping, the martinis shaken but very dry. Your door
slightly ajar, we tried to ignore the cries from across the hall,
Help me, please! Somebody help me! And sometimes an old lady,

without knocking, would wander in, a wild and vacant look in her eyes.
You still wrote poems: about a woman dying, about the news,
until you could bear the news no longer and the screen went
     dark forever.

You were like a tree, a winter tree, still bare as spring took hold.
You pretended not to mind as Time unleaved you, stealing away
walks, then eyes, then all your friends. Ingenious, eyes closed,

you time-traveled, surprising me with your near-perfect recall
of Keats and Millay, poems you'd learned by heart as a girl.
One day a friend brought you a curling willow, a gaunt bare bouquet

that corkscrewed wildly in all directions, filling your room with energy.
How long did it hold its pose? Two years? Three? It was then
that I began to wonder about it all. Was there a plan? A great design?

Or was pain simply random and continual? The last time I saw you
there was no champagne or laughter. A trip was in the offing.
You would travel light, without valise or passport.

I held your hand but didn't speak. I wish now I had stayed longer.
And now your room is empty, or worse, filled with a stranger's things.
O where, I want to know, is that curling willow now?

Photo of You Disappearing

Mt. Charleston, Nevada

for my mother

Seven years ago, you stood at the top of a mountain,
solitary in the snow. In faded jeans and windbreaker,
you smiled, or tried to smile, as a friend snapped a photo.
You had gotten the news a month before, a clouded X-ray,
then a scan, and now behind you (or ahead?) a range
of snow-covered mountains, pine trees pointing up toward
frail wisps of cloud, the sky blue cobalt bleeding into black.

Are ends like beginnings? At your service,
the minister said, *She fixed her eyes upon that shining shore.*
If I climbed the mountain, would I find the trail you took?
Would your footsteps lead me to a pass that opens west,
always west, where you went on alone, no turning back?
I stare at the picture that tells me everything and nothing.
You are smiling. The air is perfectly clear.

The Watchman

Darkness falls.
A winding trail zigs this way
and that up the mountain,
only a lantern here, there,
to mark a traveler's progress,
and then the lanterns, one by one,
go out, and it is night again.

The night is a scroll.
The moon and the stars hang there,
more permanent than we are.
And *he* is there, the watchman
watching over all, as certainly
as the moon and stars are.
If a wall is scaled, a window
silently raised by a hand
meaning to harm, the watchman
will sound the alarm.

Questions remain unanswered.
What is behind the scroll?
On what nail does it hang?
Who hammered the nail into the wall?

If the sleeper awakes too suddenly,
will the slender thread
holding it all together
be severed? All is a mystery.
It is simple to simply believe.
Or not simple at all.

The night is long,
but the watchman never sleeps.
He listens and waits,
waits to awaken us all.
There must be love in what he does,
because he does it alone,
no watchman there who watches over him.

Triptych for Rumi

The operation was a success, the incision clean. The heart, held in the cupped hands of the Surgeon, brought back to life. The heart! Like a hungry bird in the nest, open-mouthed and trembling.

And now, stitched back together again, you go on, you go on, you who have eyes for everything, nothing. Your life a mantle around your shoulders you toss aside, a heavy mantle you have no use for.

Some believe, some do not believe. You cry out, *I am less than the dust!* Or again, *I am the prodigal lost to herself, now found!* But who, in an empty house, hears you? You laugh and you weep until laughter and weeping are one.

The wound will leave a scar, the scar will be a line inscribed into the flesh forever. In the darkest night, it will be there to touch and wonder at.

Now what do you fear, what do you pray for? For the whirlwind, there on the horizon, that waits to take you in?

You! Speechless, deprived, and on your knees.

~ ~ ~

The rose, in its crimson, swirling coat, knows what it knows. It waits and it listens. It listens and says nothing.

The nothing that is everything, it thinks. *An unfolding that is a dying.* And so, alone in the room, it unburdens itself. It beckons and wavers like a flame, dancing the dance of change.

Another night, it will lead the procession, it will burn like the brightest candle, illuminating the room's four corners.

Clipping and pruning, you might make it your own. You might carry it with you everywhere, a single rose, inexplicable. And if you did, would it yield up its secrets? Would it tell you everything?

It is the unseen pearl, the heart's heart, a dream so exquisite it leaves you gasping and broken.

It exists because you exist.

The ephemeral does not escape it. Look how the wind scatters its petals, leaving a space of bright emptiness.

Foolish or true, the rose blooms only for you.

~ ~ ~

Eddies and ripples! A stick muddies the water, breaking the mirror. You look down but the face you would touch is shattered, the original face.

You have crossed the great desert to cup this water in your hands but look how it slips through your anxious fingers into the thirsty ground.

A blind woman, feeling for floating leaves and twigs, exclaims, *I see!* She holds out her open hands, marveling at how the light shines on them.

And now the third, the necessary third, appears: the white-robed stranger carrying a dipper that flashes in the sun. O water of life! Eternal flowing water!

What you do not understand, you understand. No one is immortal. You will never die.

~ ~ ~

Moment Vanishing

Now, in the quietude of evening, the dove comes.
It does not flash its feathers, does not
make a sound, but feeds on what the finches
leave behind. How little it needs.
A few hard seeds. A drop of water.

It is late summer. It is always
late summer here. The air is hot and dry.
Brown leaves lie like hands in the yard.
There is no place to turn. No place to stop.
We are hurried along, pushed farther into our lives.

Moments are vanishing all over the earth
as bombs explode, the victim is hooded,
great populations scatter on endless dust roads.
It is too much. We avert our eyes.
We wait like children for the coming of the dove.

And if I were allowed a question,
one question, of the evening dove
who asks for nothing, whose pleasure
is a few small seeds, whose heart I covet,
I would ask, *O what will I become?*

Back Yard

It didn't rain.
And it didn't rain.
And it didn't rain.
Returning, after a month away,
from a place up north,
we saw the parched and dying yard,
the hose coiled like a snake.

As if the present were past,
I walk from this thing to that,
touching dry leaves.
Here is my daughter's herb garden
where we buried the snail.
Here is the dogwood
that bloomed when T. was dying.
Here is the sunflower, ravaged by July,
and here is the rose of Sharon
coming, in August, into its own.
Here. Here. And here.
The arbor. The wisteria.
The bamboo, tenacious as ever.
The empty swing, motionless in the heat.

I unwind the coiled hose
and turn the water on,
watching it stream into the ground.
Everything is a mouth,
thirsty and unappeasable.

With each step, I move farther
into the future wondering,
How will I ever leave all this?
How? How does one ever leave?
I am the water-bearer.
I cannot die!

Author's Note

Elizabeth Spires (b. 1952 in Lancaster, Ohio) is the author of five previous collections of poetry: *Globe, Swan's Island, Annonciade, Worldling,* and *Now the Green Blade Rises.* She has also written six books for children, including *The Mouse of Amherst* and *I Heard God Talking to Me: William Edmondson and His Stone Carvings* (forthcoming in 2009), and edited *The Instant of Knowing: Lectures, Criticism, and Occasional Prose* by Josephine Jacobsen.

Spires has been the recipient of the Amy Lowell Travelling Poetry Scholarship, a Whiting Writer's Award, a Guggenheim Fellowship, two fellowships from the National Endowment for the Arts, the Witter Bynner Prize from the American Academy of Arts and Letters, two Ohioana Book Awards, and the Maryland Author Award from the Maryland Library Association. Her poems have appeared in *The New Yorker, Poetry, The Atlantic, The New Republic, American Poetry Review, The New Criterion, The Paris Review,* and many other literary magazines and anthologies.

She lives in Baltimore with her husband and daughter and is a professor of English at Goucher College where she holds a Chair for Distinguished Achievement.